Practical
Desserts

p^3

This is a P³ Book
First published in 2003

P³
Queen Street House
4 Queen Street
Bath BA1 1HE, UK

ISBN: 1-40540-933-9

Printed in China

NOTE

Cup measurements in this book are for American cups.
This book also uses imperial and metric measurements. Follow the same units
of measurement throughout; do not mix imperial and metric.
All spoon measurements are level: teaspoons are assumed to be 5 ml, and
tablespoons are assumed to be 15 ml. Unless otherwise stated,
milk is assumed to be whole milk, eggs and individual vegetables such as potatoes
are medium, and pepper is freshly ground black pepper.

The nutritional information provided for each recipe is per serving or per person.
Optional ingredients, variations, or serving suggestions have not been
included in the calculations. The times given for each recipe are an approximate
guide only because the preparation times may differ according to the techniques used by
different people and the cooking times may vary as a result of the type of oven used.

Recipes using raw or very lightly cooked eggs should be
avoided by infants, the elderly, pregnant women, convalescents,
and anyone suffering from an illness.

Contents

Introduction 4

Honeyed Rice Desserts 6

Fruity Queen of Puddings 7

Quick Syrup Sponge 8

Mixed Fruit Crust 9

Bread & Butter Pudding 10

Spiced Steamed Sponge 11

Fruity Crêpe Bundles 12

Traditional Apple Pie 13

Baked Semolina Dessert 14

Cherry Clafoutis 15

Fruit Brûlée 16

Tropical Salad 17

Orange Syllabub 18

New Age Spotted Dick 19

Mascarpone Cheesecake 20

Egg Mousse with Marsala 21

Quick Tiramisu 22

Summer Fruit Dessert 23

Panettone with Strawberries 24

Vanilla Ice Cream 25

Mango Mousse 26

Exotic Fruit Crêpes 27

Coconut Cream Molds 28

Banana & Mango Tart 29

Almond Trifles 30

Mini Florentines 31

Apple Fritters 32

Introduction

For anyone with a sweet tooth, no meal is complete without a sumptuous dessert to finish it off. Desserts come in a multitude of forms, and everyone has their favorite—whether it be the taste of Italy in a tiramisu, a taste of Asia in an exotic fruit salad, or the taste of America in a traditional apple pie. All tastes have been catered for in this book.

A historical role

Desserts have enjoyed pride of place on the table through history, around the world. From rich chocolate desserts, which followed the arrival and widespread use of the cocoa bean in western Europe in the eighteenth century, to beautifully simple yet delicious fruit salads made from the fresh fruit of local trees, a dessert is always something special. Desserts have always held an individual place in a meal: they signify a luxury—even in the richest of households. Traditionally the dessert arrives at the end of the meal when people can barely eat any more, yet most manage to eat their share of the pièce de résistance, which may be served with much pomp and ceremony. Ornate dishes, decorative tableware, and the best cutlery are frequently reserved for serving this part of the meal. A successful dessert makes its creator proud and delights everyone.

Spoil yourself

Desserts are a real opportunity to spoil the gourmand in you. You can impress family and friends, make tempting treats for special occasions, birthdays or dinner parties—or simply spoil yourself. With very little effort you can create stunning masterpieces that enhance your table as well as providing a delicious end to a meal.

Healthy eating

For those who crave a warm winter dessert or a summer trifle without piling on the calories, recipes have been found that the health-conscious can enjoy. Fruit is an excellent ingredient for lowfat desserts because it is fat-free and naturally sweet. The huge variety of fruit available in supermarkets and grocery stores means that many different flavors and textures can be achieved.

Vegetarian desserts

Vegetarians can enjoy a wealth of dishes from the dessert menu, although strict vegetarians should avoid puddings that contain gelatin. From rich syrup sponges and fruity brûlées, to bread and butter pudding and delicious crêpes, these delicious creations will have all the vegetarians in your household clamoring for more.

Family favorites

This book contains selections of all of your favorite desserts, from sweet rice puddings and delicious apple pies, to irresistible trifles and mouthwatering chocolate biscuits. A sumptuous treat can be found for any time of day or year. Everyone in your household will love the desserts featured within these pages. Some are ideal for parties, while others will be enjoyed after meals or in lunch boxes. Among these irresistible desserts are some new adaptations of old snack-time favorites.

Cooking times and techniques

Some desserts may take a while to prepare, others may need to spend time in the oven to cook, and others

will need to be left to cool or stand before serving. Make sure you read the recipe through when planning your meal. Despite the fact that the dessert is probably the last dish to arrive on your table, it may be best to prepare it, or begin cooking it first. And remember, all ovens do vary, so alter suggested cooking times in accordance with your oven and keep checking the progress of the dessert when possible.

The following terms are common in dessert recipes and these definitions will help you achieve the best results:

Blending This involves the mixing together of two or more ingredients with a spoon, beater, or electric blender, until they are completely combined.

Folding This is used to carefully combine light, airy ingredients (such as egg whites) with heavier mixtures (such as cream) without losing too much of the air contained in the lighter one. Folding is a delicate technique where the lighter mixture is placed on top of the heavier one in a bowl sufficiently large to incorporate all the ingredients, with enough room to mix. A rubber spatula is often used to fold ingredients and the mixing should be done slowly and carefully. Cutting down through the mixture from the back of the bowl towards the front and lifting the bottom mixture over the top, whilst turning the bowl a quarter turn after each stroke, is the best method of folding ingredients together. Continue until the two different mixtures are fully combined.

Creaming This method is used to combine ingredients until they are smooth and "creamy" in texture. Sugar and butter are two ingredients that are frequently combined in this way. The ingredients are creamed when you can no longer see the different constituents and they have formed a homogeneous paste; electric mixers can greatly speed up this process.

Greasing This is essential in baking to stop ingredients from sticking to their containers during cooking. Butter is ideal for greasing cake pans or cookie sheets. Use waxed paper or butter wrappers covered in fat to rub the bottom and sides of the pan or sheet, leaving a thin coating of grease. If asked to grease and flour the container, apply the grease and then sprinkle flour over the top. Shake the container to ensure a complete and even covering and then tip the pan or sheet upside down over the sink to remove any excess flour.

Beating The most common way to mix ingredients, beating simply means combining all the ingredients using a spoon, fork, or mixer by stirring rapidly in a circular motion. Electric mixers save a lot of time and energy and are much better than beating ingredients by hand.

How to make the best desserts

- Start by reading the recipe all the way through.
- Weigh all the ingredients accurately and do basic preparation, such as grating and chopping, before you start cooking.
- Basic cake-making ingredients should be kept at room temperature.
- Mixtures that are creamed should be almost white and have a "soft dropping" consistency. This can be done by hand, but using a hand-held electric mixer will save time.
- Do not remove a cake from the oven until it is fully cooked. To test if a cake is cooked, press the surface lightly with your fingertips—it should feel springy to the touch. Alternatively, insert a fine metal skewer into the center of the cake—it will come out clean if the cake is cooked through.

- Leave cakes in their pans to cool before carefully turning out onto a wire rack to cool completely.

KEY	
	Simplicity level 1–3 (1 easiest, 3 slightly harder)
	Preparation time
	Cooking time

Honeyed Rice Desserts

These small rice desserts are quite sweet, but have a marvelous flavor because of the combination of ginger, honey, and cinnamon.

NUTRITIONAL INFORMATION

Calories 199	Sugars 15g
Protein 3g	Fat 1g
Carbohydrate ...46g	Saturates 0g

10 mins

50 mins

SERVES 4

INGREDIENTS

1½ cups dessert rice

2 tbsp clear honey, plus extra
   for drizzling

large pinch of ground cinnamon

1 tbsp butter, for greasing

15 no-need-to-soak dried apricots, chopped

3 pieces preserved ginger, drained
   and chopped

8 whole no-need-to-soak dried apricots,
   to decorate

1 Put the rice in a pan and just cover with cold water. Bring to a boil, lower the heat, cover the pan, and cook for about 15 minutes, or until the water has been absorbed. Stir the honey and cinnamon into the rice.

2 Grease four ⅔-cup ramekin dishes with butter.

3 Blend the chopped dried apricots and ginger in a food processor to make a smooth paste.

4 Divide the paste into 4 equal portions and shape each into a flat circle to fit into the bottom of the ramekin dishes.

5 Divide half of the rice among the ramekin dishes and place the apricot paste on top.

6 Cover the apricot paste with the remaining rice. Cover the ramekins with waxed paper and foil and steam for 30 minutes, or until set.

7 Remove the ramekins from the steamer and let stand for 5 minutes.

8 Turn the desserts out onto warm serving plates and drizzle with honey. Decorate with dried apricots and serve.

COOK'S TIP

The desserts may be left to chill in their ramekin dishes in the refrigerator, then turned out and served with ice cream or cream.

Fruity Queen of Puddings

A delicious version of a classic British dessert, made here with fresh bananas and apricot jelly.

NUTRITIONAL INFORMATION

Calories . . . . . . .406 Sugars 60g
Protein . . . . .13g Fat 7g
Carbohydrate . . .77g Saturates 3g

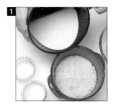

30 mins   1 hr

SERVES 4

I N G R E D I E N T S

2 cups fresh white bread crumbs

2½ cups milk

3 eggs

½ tsp vanilla extract

4 tbsp superfine sugar

2 bananas

1 tbsp lemon juice

3 tbsp apricot jelly

1 Sprinkle the bread crumbs evenly into a 4-cup casserole. Heat the milk until just lukewarm, then pour it over the bread crumbs.

2 Separate 2 of the eggs and beat the yolks with the remaining whole egg. Add to the casserole with the vanilla extract and half the sugar, stirring well to mix. Set aside for 10 minutes.

3 Bake in a preheated oven, 350°F/ 180°C, for 40 minutes, until set. Remove the dish from the oven.

4 Slice the bananas and sprinkle with the lemon juice. Spoon the apricot jelly onto the dessert and spread out to cover the surface. Arrange the banana slices on top of the apricot jelly.

5 Whisk the egg whites until stiff, then add the remaining sugar. Continue whisking until the meringue mixture is very stiff and glossy.

6 Pile the meringue mixture on top of the dessert, return to the oven, and cook for another 10–15 minutes, until the meringue is just set and golden brown. Serve immediately.

COOK'S TIP

This meringue will have a soft texture, unlike a hard meringue, which is cooked slowly for 2–3 hours until dry. Always use a grease-free bowl and whisk for beating egg whites.

Quick Syrup Sponge

You won't believe your eyes when you see just how quickly this light-as-air sponge cooks in the microwave oven!

NUTRITIONAL INFORMATION

Calories	650	Sugars	........60g
Protein	........10g	Fat	..........31g
Carbohydrate	...89g	Saturates	.......7g

🍰 15 mins 🕐 5 mins

SERVES 4

I N G R E D I E N T S

5 oz/140 g butter or margarine

4 tbsp light corn syrup

6 tbsp superfine sugar

2 eggs

1 cup self-rising flour

1 tsp baking powder

about 2 tbsp warm water

custard, to serve

1 Grease a 2¾-pint/1.5-liter heatproof bowl with a small amount of the butter or margarine. Spoon the syrup into the bowl.

2 Cream the remaining butter or margarine with the sugar, until light

and fluffy. Gradually add the eggs, beating well after each addition.

3 Sift the flour and baking powder together, then fold into the creamed mixture using a large metal spoon. Add enough water to give a soft, dropping consistency. Spoon into the heatproof bowl and level the surface.

4 Cover the bowl with microwave-safe plastic wrap, leaving a small space to let air escape. Microwave on HIGH power for 4 minutes, then remove the sponge from the microwave oven and let stand for 5 minutes, while it continues to cook.

5 Turn the sponge out onto a warm serving plate. Serve with custard.

COOK'S TIP

If you do not have a microwave oven, the sponge can be steamed. Cover the bowl with a piece of pleated baking parchment and a piece of pleated foil. Place in a pan, add boiling water, and steam for 1½ hours.

Mixed Fruit Crust

In this crusty dessert, tropical fruits are flavored with ginger and coconut, for something a little different and very tasty.

NUTRITIONAL INFORMATION

Calories	602	Sugars	........51g
Protein	.........6g	Fat	..........29g
Carbohydrate	...84g	Saturates	......11g

10 mins   50 mins

SERVES 4

I N G R E D I E N T S

2 mangoes, sliced

1 papaya, seeded and sliced

8 oz/225 g fresh pineapple, cubed

1½ tsp ground ginger

3½ oz/100 g margarine

scant ½ cup light brown sugar

1½ cups all-purpose flour

⅔ cup dry shredded coconut, plus extra
to decorate

1 Place the mangoes, papaya, and pineapple in a pan with ½ teaspoon of the ground ginger, 2 tablespoons of the margarine, and 4 tablespoons of the sugar. Cook over low heat for 10 minutes, until the fruit softens. Spoon the fruit into the bottom of a shallow ovenproof dish.

2 Combine the flour and remaining ginger. Rub in the remaining margarine, until the mixture resembles fine bread crumbs. Stir in the remaining sugar and the coconut and spoon over the fruit to cover completely.

3 Cook in a preheated oven, 350°F/180°C, for 40 minutes, or until the top is crisp. Decorate with a sprinkling of dry shredded coconut and then serve immediately.

Bread & Butter Pudding

Everyone has their own favorite recipe for this dish. This one has added marmalade and grated apples for a really rich and unique taste.

NUTRITIONAL INFORMATION

Calories 427   Sugars 63g
Protein ....9g   Fat 13g
Carbohydrate ...74g   Saturates 7g

45 mins   1 hr

SERVES 6

INGREDIENTS

4 tbsp butter, softened

4–5 slices white or whole-wheat bread

4 tbsp chunky orange marmalade

grated zest of 1 lemon

½–¾ cup golden raisins

¼ cup chopped candied peel

1 tsp ground cinnamon or allspice

1 cooking apple, peeled, cored, and coarsely grated

scant ½ cup brown sugar

3 eggs

generous 2 cups milk

2 tbsp raw brown sugar

  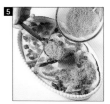

1 Use the softened butter to grease an ovenproof dish and to spread on the slices of bread, then spread the bread with the marmalade.

2 Place a layer of bread in the bottom of the dish and sprinkle with the lemon zest, half the golden raisins, half the candied peel, half the spice, all of the apple, and half the brown sugar. Add another layer of bread, cutting it so that it fits the dish.

3 Sprinkle over most of the remaining golden raisins and all the remaining candied peel, with all the remaining spice and brown sugar, scattering them evenly over the bread. Top with a final layer of bread, again cutting to fit the dish.

4 Lightly beat together the eggs and milk and then carefully strain the mixture over the bread in the dish. If you have enough time, let the dessert stand for 20–30 minutes.

5 Sprinkle the raw brown sugar over the top and scatter over the remaining golden raisins. Cook in a preheated oven, 400°F/200°C, for 50–60 minutes, until risen and golden brown. Serve immediately or let cool and serve cold.

Spiced Steamed Sponge

Steamed sponges are irresistible on a winter day, but the texture of this sponge is so light it can be served throughout the year.

NUTRITIONAL INFORMATION

Calories	488	Sugars	........56g
Protein	.........5g	Fat	..........19g
Carbohydrate	...78g	Saturates	.......4g

15 mins   1½ hrs

SERVES 6

INGREDIENTS

5 oz/140 g butter or margarine, plus extra for greasing

2 tbsp light corn syrup, plus extra to serve

½ cup superfine or light brown sugar

2 eggs

scant 1½ cups self-rising flour

¾ tsp ground cinnamon or allspice

grated zest of 1 orange

1 tbsp orange juice

¾ cup golden raisins

2 pieces preserved ginger, finely chopped

1 eating apple, peeled, cored, and coarsely grated

1 Thoroughly grease a 1½-pint/850-ml heatproof bowl. Put the light corn syrup into the bowl.

2 Cream the butter or margarine with the sugar, until very light and fluffy and pale in color. Beat in the eggs, one at a time, following each with a spoonful of the flour.

3 Sift the remaining flour with the cinnamon or allspice and fold into the mixture, followed by the orange zest and juice. Fold in the golden raisins, then the ginger and apple.

4 Turn the mixture into the heatproof bowl and level the top. Cover with a piece of pleated, greased baking parchment, tucking the edges under the rim of the bowl.

5 Cover with a sheet of pleated foil. Tie securely in place with string, with a piece of string tied over the top of the bowl for a handle to make it easy to lift out of the pan.

6 Put the bowl into a pan half-filled with boiling water, cover, and steam for 1½ hours, adding more boiling water to the pan as necessary during cooking.

7 To serve the spiced steamed sponge, remove the foil and the baking parchment, turn the sponge out onto a warmed serving plate, and serve at once in slices with a little of the light corn syrup poured over the top.

Fruity Crêpe Bundles

This unusual crêpe is filled with a sweet cream flavored with ginger, nuts, and apricots and served with a raspberry and orange sauce.

NUTRITIONAL INFORMATION	
Calories 610	Sugars 60g
Protein 19g	Fat 20g
Carbohydrate . . .94g	Saturates 5g

15 mins   35 mins

SERVES 2

I N G R E D I E N T S

BATTER

½ cup all-purpose flour

pinch of salt

¼ tsp ground cinnamon

1 egg

generous ½ cup milk

white vegetable shortening, for cooking

FILLING

1½ tsp all-purpose flour, strained

1½ tsp cornstarch

1 tbsp superfine sugar

1 egg

⅔ cup milk

4 tbsp chopped nuts

scant ¼ cup ready-to-eat dried apricots, chopped

1 piece of preserved or candied ginger, finely chopped

SAUCE

3 tbsp raspberry preserve

4½ tsp orange juice

finely grated zest of ¼ orange

1 To make the batter, sift the flour, salt, and cinnamon into a bowl and make a well in the center. Add the egg and milk and gradually beat in, until smooth.

2 Melt a little shortening in a medium skillet. Pour in half the batter. Cook for 2 minutes, until golden, then turn and cook the other side for about 1 minute, until browned. Set aside and make a second crêpe.

3 For the filling, beat the flour with the cornstarch, sugar, and egg. Gently heat the milk in a pan, then beat 2 tablespoons into the flour mixture. Transfer the flour mixture to the pan and cook gently, stirring constantly, until thick. Remove from the heat, cover with baking parchment to prevent a skin from forming, and let cool.

4 Beat the chopped nuts and apricots, and the preserved ginger into the cooled mixture, and then put a heaping tablespoonful in the center of each crêpe. Gather and squeeze the edges together to make a bundle. Place in an ovenproof dish and then bake in a preheated oven, 350°F/180°C, for 15–20 minutes, until hot and golden but not too brown.

5 To make the sauce, melt the preserve gently with the orange juice, then strain. Return to a clean pan with the orange zest and heat through. Serve with the crêpes.

Traditional Apple Pie

This two-crust apple pie can be served either hot or cold. The apples can be flavored with other spices or with grated citrus zest.

NUTRITIONAL INFORMATION

Calories	577	Sugars	........36g
Protein	.........6g	Fat	..........28g
Carbohydrate	...80g	Saturates	.......9g

55 mins · 50 mins

SERVES 6

INGREDIENTS

1¾–2¼ lb/800 g–1 kg cooking apples, peeled, cored, and sliced

scant ¾ cup brown or white sugar, plus extra for sprinkling

½–1 tsp ground cinnamon, allspice, or ground ginger

1–2 tbsp water (optional)

SHORTCRUST PIE DOUGH

3 cups all-purpose flour

pinch of salt

6 tbsp butter or margarine

6 tbsp white vegetable shortening

about 6 tbsp cold water

beaten egg or milk, to glaze

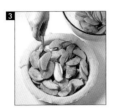

8-9-inch/20-23-cm deep pie plate or shallow pie pan.

1 To make the pie dough, sift the flour and salt into a mixing bowl. Add the butter or margarine with the shortening and rub in with the fingertips, until the mixture resembles fine bread crumbs. Add the water and gather the mixture together into a dough. Wrap the dough in foil and chill for 30 minutes.

2 Roll out almost two-thirds of the pie dough thinly and use it to line an

3 For the filling, mix the apples with the sugar and spice and pack into the pie shell; the filling can come up above the rim. Add the water if needed, particularly if the apples are a dry variety.

4 Roll out the remaining pie dough to form a lid. Dampen the edges of the pie rim with water and position the lid, pressing the edges firmly together. Trim the edges and crimp them decoratively.

5 Use the leftover trimmings to cut out leaves or other shapes to decorate the top of the pie: dampen them and attach them to the top. Glaze the top of the pie with beaten egg or milk, use a knife to make 1–2 slits in the top, then put the pie on a cookie sheet.

6 Bake the pie in a preheated oven, 425°F/220°C, for 20 minutes, then lower the temperature to 350°F/180°C and cook for 30 minutes, or until the pastry is a light golden brown. Serve the pie hot or cold, sprinkled with brown or white sugar.

Baked Semolina Dessert

Succulent plums simmered in orange juice and spices complement this rich and creamy semolina dessert perfectly.

NUTRITIONAL INFORMATION

Calories	304	Sugars	.......32g
Protein	.........9g	Fat	..........12g
Carbohydrate	...43g	Saturates	.......4g

 5 mins   🕐 45 mins

SERVES 4

I N G R E D I E N T S

2 tbsp butter or margarine

2½ cups milk

finely pared rind and juice of 1 orange

⅓ cup semolina

pinch of grated nutmeg

2 tbsp superfine sugar

1 egg, beaten

TO DECORATE

small piece of butter

grated nutmeg

SPICED PLUMS

8 oz/225 g plums, halved and pitted

⅔ cup orange juice

2 tbsp superfine sugar

½ tsp allspice

1 Grease a 4-cup ovenproof dish with a little of the butter or margarine. Put the milk, the remaining butter or margarine, and the orange rind in a pan. Sprinkle in the semolina and bring to a boil over low heat, stirring constantly. Simmer gently for about 2–3 minutes. Remove the pan from the heat.

2 Add the nutmeg, orange juice, and sugar, stirring well. Add the beaten egg and stir to mix.

3 Transfer the mixture to the prepared dish and bake in a preheated oven, 375°F/190°C, for about 30 minutes, until lightly browned.

4 To make the spiced plums, put the plums, orange juice, sugar, and spice into a pan and simmer gently for about 10 minutes, until the plums are just tender. Remove the pan from the heat and set aside to cool slightly.

5 Top the dessert with a piece of butter and a sprinkling of grated nutmeg, and serve with the spiced plums.

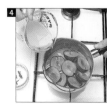

Cherry Clafoutis

This is a hot dessert that is simple and quick to put together. Try the batter with other fruits—apricots and plums are particularly delicious.

NUTRITIONAL INFORMATION

Calories 261	Sugars 24g
Protein 10g	Fat 6g
Carbohydrate . . .40g	Saturates 3g

🍮 10 mins   🕐 40 mins

SERVES 6

I N G R E D I E N T S

1 cup all-purpose flour

4 eggs, lightly beaten

2 tbsp superfine sugar

pinch of salt

2½ cups milk

butter, for greasing

1 lb/450 g pitted black cherries, fresh or canned

3 tbsp brandy

1 tbsp sugar, to decorate

3 Thoroughly grease a 3-pint/1.75-liter ovenproof serving dish with butter and pour in about half of the batter.

4 Spoon over the cherries and pour the remaining batter over the top. Sprinkle the brandy over the batter.

5 Bake in a preheated oven, 350°F/180°C, for 40 minutes, or until risen and golden brown.

6 Remove from the oven and sprinkle over the sugar just before serving. Serve the clafoutis warm.

1 Sift the flour into a large mixing bowl. Make a well in the center and add the eggs, sugar, and salt. Gradually draw in the flour from around the edges and whisk until incorporated.

2 Pour in the milk and whisk the batter thoroughly, until very smooth.

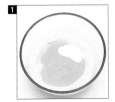

Fruit Brûlée

This is a cheat's brûlée, in that yogurt is used to cover a layer of fruit, before being sprinkled with sugar and broiled.

NUTRITIONAL INFORMATION

Calories 311	Sugars 48g	
Protein 7g	Fat 11g	
Carbohydrate . . .48g	Saturates 7g	

🍲 1¼ hrs   🕐 15 mins

SERVES 4

I N G R E D I E N T S

4 plums, pitted and sliced

2 cooking apples, peeled and sliced

2 tbsp water

1 tsp ground ginger

2½ cups strained plain yogurt

2 tbsp confectioners' sugar, sifted

1 tsp almond extract

⅓ cup raw brown sugar

1 Put the plums and apples in a pan with 2 tablespoons of water and cook for 7–10 minutes, until tender but not mushy. Set aside to cool, then stir in the ground ginger.

2 Using a slotted spoon, lift out the fruit and spoon into the bottom of a shallow, heatproof serving dish.

3 Combine the yogurt, confectioners' sugar, and almond extract and spoon onto the fruit to cover.

4 Sprinkle the raw brown sugar over the top of the yogurt mixture and cook under a hot broiler for 3–4 minutes, or until the sugar has melted and formed a crust.

5 Set aside to chill in the refrigerator for 1 hour before serving.

Tropical Salad

Here, ripe tropical fruits are blended with rum and orange juice.
You could serve in the shells of baby pineapples for a stunning effect.

NUTRITIONAL INFORMATION

Calories 69   Sugars 13g
Protein ....1g   Fat 0.3g
Carbohydrate ...14g   Saturates 0g

 10 mins   ⏱ 0 mins

SERVES 8

INGREDIENTS

1 papaya

2 tbsp fresh orange juice

3 tbsp rum

2 bananas

2 guavas

1 small pineapple or 2 baby pineapples

2 passion fruit

pineapple leaves, to decorate

scooped-out baby pineapple shells,
   to serve (optional)

1 Cut the papaya in half and remove the seeds. Peel and slice the flesh into a bowl.

2 Pour the orange juice over the papaya in the bowl, then pour over the rum.

3 Slice the bananas, peel and slice the guavas, and add them to the bowl.

4 Cut the top and bottom from the pineapple, then cut off the skin.

5 Slice the pineapple flesh, discard the core, cut into pieces, and add to the bowl.

6 Halve the passion fruit, scoop out the flesh with a teaspoon, add to the bowl, and stir well to mix.

7 Spoon the fruit salad into glass bowls and decorate with pineapple leaves. Alternatively, serve the fruit in scooped-out baby pineapple shells.

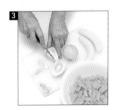

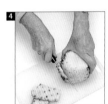

COOK'S TIP

Guavas have a heavenly smell when ripe—their scent will fill a whole room. They should yield to gentle pressure when ripe, and their skins should be yellow. The canned varieties are very good and have a pink tinge to the flesh.

Orange Syllabub

This is a zesty, creamy whip made from yogurt and milk with a hint of orange, served with light and luscious sweet sponge cakes.

NUTRITIONAL INFORMATION

Calories .... .464 Sugars .... .74g
Protein ....22g Fat 5g
Carbohydrate ...89g Saturates 2g

1½ hrs   10 mins

SERVES 4

INGREDIENTS

4 oranges

2½ cups lowfat unsweetened yogurt

6 tbsp lowfat skim milk powder

4 tbsp superfine sugar

1 tbsp grated orange zest

4 tbsp orange juice

2 egg whites

strips of orange zest, to decorate

SPONGE HEARTS

2 medium eggs

6 tbsp superfine sugar

⅓ cup all-purpose flour

⅓ cup whole-wheat flour

1 tbsp hot water

1 tsp confectioners' sugar

1 Slice off the tops and bottoms of the oranges and remove the skin. Then cut out the segments, removing the zest and membranes between each one. Divide the orange segments between 4 dessert glasses, then chill.

2 In a mixing bowl, combine the yogurt, milk powder, sugar, orange zest, and orange juice. Cover and chill for 1 hour. Whisk the egg whites until stiff, then fold into the yogurt mixture. Spoon onto the orange slices and chill for an hour. Decorate with strips of orange zest.

3 To make the sponge hearts, line a 6 x 10-inch/15 x 25-cm baking pan with baking parchment. Whisk the eggs and superfine sugar together, until thick and pale. Sift the flours, then fold into the eggs, using a large metal spoon, adding the hot water at the same time.

4 Pour into the prepared pan and bake in a preheated oven at 425°F/220°C for 9–10 minutes, until golden on top and firm to the touch.

5 Turn the sponge out onto a sheet of baking parchment. Using a 2-inch/5-cm heart-shape cutter, stamp out hearts from the sponge. Transfer to a wire rack to cool. Lightly dust with confectioners' sugar before serving with the syllabub.

New Age Spotted Dick

This is a deliciously moist lowfat dessert. The sauce is in the center of the dessert, and will spill out when the sponge is cut.

NUTRITIONAL INFORMATION

Calories	529	Sugars	........41g
Protein	.........9g	Fat	..........31g
Carbohydrate	...58g	Saturates	......4g

25 mins   1¼ hrs

SERVES 6–8

INGREDIENTS

1 cup raisins

¼ cup water

½ cup corn oil, plus extra for greasing

½ cup superfine sugar

⅓ cup ground almonds

2 eggs, lightly beaten

scant 1½ cups self-rising flour

SAUCE

½ cup walnuts, chopped

⅔ cup ground almonds

1¼ cups lowfat milk

4 tbsp granulated sugar

1 Put the raisins in a pan with ¼ cup water. Bring to a boil, then remove from the heat. Let steep for 10 minutes, then drain.

2 Whisk together the oil, sugar, and ground almonds, until thick and syrupy; this will need about 8 minutes of beating (on medium speed if using an electric whisk).

3 Add the eggs, one at a time, beating well after each addition. Combine the flour and raisins. Stir into the mixture.

4 Brush a 4-cup/1-liter heatproof bowl with oil, or line with baking parchment.

5 Put all the sauce ingredients into a pan. Bring to a boil, stir, and simmer for 10 minutes.

6 Transfer the sponge mixture to the greased bowl and pour on the hot sauce. Place on a cookie sheet.

7 Bake in a preheated oven at 350°F/ 180°C for about 1 hour, or until well risen. Lay a piece of baking parchment across the top of the sponge if it starts to brown too quickly.

8 Let cool for 2–3 minutes in the bowl before turning out onto a warm serving plate.

COOK'S TIP
Always soak raisins before baking them, because they retain their moisture nicely and you taste their full flavor instead of biting on a dried-out raisin.

Mascarpone Cheesecake

Lemon and ginger give this baked cheesecake a marvelously tangy flavor. Ricotta cheese could be used as an alternative.

NUTRITIONAL INFORMATION

Calories 327	Sugars 25g	
Protein 9g	Fat 18g	
Carbohydrate ... 33g	Saturates 11g	

 15 mins   50 mins

SERVES 4

I N G R E D I E N T S

1½ tbsp unsalted butter, plus extra for greasing

5½ oz/150 g ginger cookies, crushed

1 oz/25 g preserved ginger, chopped

1 lb 2 oz/500 g mascarpone cheese

finely grated rind and juice of 2 lemons

3½ oz/100 g superfine sugar

2 large eggs, separated

fruit coulis (see Cook's Tip), to serve

1 Grease a 10-inch/25-cm springform cake pan or loose-bottomed pan and line the bottom with baking parchment. Brush the parchment with butter.

2 Melt the butter in a pan and stir in the crushed cookies and chopped ginger. Use the mixture to line the pan, pressing the mixture about ¼ inch/5 mm up the sides.

COOK'S TIP

Make a delicious fruit coulis by cooking 14 oz/400 g fruit, such as blueberries, for 5 minutes with 2 tablespoons of water. Strain, then stir in 1 tablespoon (or more to taste) of sifted confectioners' sugar. Cool before serving.

3 Beat together the cheese, lemon rind and juice, sugar, and egg yolks, until quite smooth.

4 Whisk the egg whites until they are stiff, then fold into the cheese and lemon mixture.

5 Pour the mixture into the prepared pan and bake in a preheated oven, 350°F/180°C, for 35–45 minutes, until it is just set. Do not worry if it cracks or sinks—this is quite normal.

6 Remove the cheesecake from the oven. Leave in the pan to cool completely.

7 Serve the cheesecake with a fruit coulis (see Cook's Tip).

Egg Mousse with Marsala

This warm mousse is known as *zabaglione* in Italy. It will not keep, so make it fresh and serve immediately.

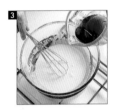

NUTRITIONAL INFORMATION

Calories	158	Sugars 29g
Protein	. . . . .1g	Fat 1g
Carbohydrate	. . .29g	Saturates 0.2g

🍓 15 mins   🕐 0 mins

SERVES 4

INGREDIENTS

5 egg yolks

½ cup superfine sugar

⅔ cup Marsala wine or sweet sherry

fresh fruit or amaretti cookies,
    to serve (optional)

1 Place the egg yolks in a mixing bowl. Add the sugar to the egg yolks and whisk until the mixture is thick and very pale and has doubled in volume.

2 Place the bowl containing the egg mixture over a pan of simmering water.

3 Add the Marsala wine or sherry to the egg mixture and continue whisking, until the mixture becomes warm and foamy. This process may take as long as 10 minutes.

4 Pour the mixture, which should now be foamy and light, into 4 wine glasses.

5 Serve the mousse warm with fresh fruit or amaretti cookies, if you desire.

COOK'S TIP

Any other type of liqueur may be used instead of the Marsala wine or sweet sherry, if you prefer. Serve soft fruits, such as strawberries or raspberries, with the zabaglione—it is a delicious combination.

Quick Tiramisu

This quick version of one of the most popular Italian desserts is ready in minutes.

NUTRITIONAL INFORMATION	
Calories 387	Sugars 17g
Protein 9g	Fat 28g
Carbohydrate ...22g	Saturates 15g

 15 mins   0 mins

SERVES 4

I N G R E D I E N T S

1 cup mascarpone or fullfat soft cheese

1 egg, separated

2 tbsp plain yogurt

2 tbsp superfine sugar

2 tbsp dark rum

2 tbsp strong black coffee

8 ladyfingers

2 tbsp grated dark chocolate

1 Put the cheese in a large bowl, add the egg yolk and yogurt, and beat with a wooden spoon until smooth.

2 Whisk the egg white until stiff but not dry, then whisk in the sugar and carefully fold into the cheese mixture.

COOK'S TIP

Mascarpone is an Italian soft cream cheese made from cow's milk. It has a rich, silky smooth texture and a deliciously creamy flavor. It can be eaten as it is with fresh fruits or flavored with coffee or chocolate.

3 Spoon half of the mixture into 4 sundae glasses.

4 Mix together the rum and coffee in a shallow dish. Dip the ladyfingers into the rum mixture, break them in half, or into smaller pieces if necessary, and divide among the glasses.

5 Stir any remaining coffee mixture into the remaining cheese and spoon over the top.

6 Sprinkle with grated chocolate. Serve immediately or chill until required.

Summer Fruit Dessert

A sweet cream cheese dessert that complements the tartness of fresh summer fruits very well.

NUTRITIONAL INFORMATION

Calories	725	Sugars	.......36g
Protein	........10g	Fat	.........59g
Carbohydrate	...36g	Saturates	......36g

5 mins, plus
1 hr 20 mins
chilling

0 mins

SERVES 4

I N G R E D I E N T S

1 lb/450 g mascarpone cheese

4 egg yolks, lightly beaten

½ cup superfine sugar

14 oz/400 g frozen summer fruits, such as raspberries and red currants

whole red currants, to decorate

amaretti cookies, to serve

1 Place the mascarpone cheese in a large mixing bowl and beat with a wooden spoon, until smooth.

2 Stir the egg yolks and sugar into the mascarpone cheese, mixing well. Cover and let the mixture chill in the refrigerator for about 1 hour.

3 Spoon a layer of the chilled mascarpone mixture into the bottom of 4 individual serving dishes. Spoon a layer of the frozen summer fruits on top. Repeat the layers in the same order, reserving some of the mascarpone mixture for the top.

4 Let the mascarpone mousses chill in the refrigerator for about 20 minutes. The fruits should still be slightly frozen. Decorate with whole red currants and serve with amaretti cookies.

VARIATION

Try adding 3 tablespoons of your favorite liqueur to the mascarpone cheese mixture in step 1, if you prefer.

Panettone with Strawberries

Panettone is a sweet Italian bread. It is delicious toasted on the grill and topped with mascarpone and marinated strawberries.

NUTRITIONAL INFORMATION

Calories 475   Sugars 20g
Protein ....7g   Fat 31g
Carbohydrate ...36g   Saturates 19g

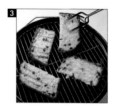

5 mins, plus 30 mins chilling   2 mins

SERVES 4

I N G R E D I E N T S

8 oz/225 g strawberries

2 tbsp superfine sugar

6 tbsp Marsala wine

½ tsp ground cinnamon

4 slices panettone

4 tbsp mascarpone cheese

1 Hull the strawberries, then slice them from top to bottom and place in a bowl. Add the sugar, Marsala wine, and ground cinnamon to the strawberries.

2 Toss the strawberries in the sugar and cinnamon mixture, until they are well coated. Let chill in the refrigerator for at least 30 minutes.

3 When ready to serve, transfer the slices of panettone to a rack set over medium–hot coals. Grill the panettone for about 1 minute on each side, or until golden brown. Alternatively, it can be cooked under a broiler.

4 Remove the panettone from the grill and transfer to serving plates. Top with the mascarpone cheese and marinated strawberries, and serve immediately.

Vanilla Ice Cream

Italy is synonymous with ice cream. This homemade version of real vanilla ice cream is absolutely delicious and so easy to make.

NUTRITIONAL INFORMATION

Calories	652	Sugars	........33g
Protein	.........8g	Fat	..........55g
Carbohydrate	...33g	Saturates	......32g

5 mins, plus 1 hr cooling

10 mins

SERVES 4–6

I N G R E D I E N T S

2½ cups heavy cream

1 vanilla bean

pared zest of 1 lemon

4 eggs, beaten

2 egg yolks

6 oz/175 g superfine sugar

1 Place the cream in a heavy pan and heat gently, whisking. Add the vanilla bean, lemon zest, eggs, and egg yolks and heat until the mixture reaches just below boiling point.

2 Lower the heat and cook for 8–10 minutes, whisking the mixture continuously, until thickened. Stir the sugar into the cream mixture, set aside, and let cool, then strain the cream mixture through a strainer.

3 Slit open the vanilla bean, scoop out the seeds, and stir into the cream.

4 Pour the mixture into a shallow freezing container with a lid and freeze overnight, until set.

COOK'S TIP

For a superfine ice cream, beat the mixture when just freezing, and then freeze again.

Mango Mousse

This is a light, softly set, and tangy mousse, which is perfect for clearing the palate after a meal of mixed flavors.

NUTRITIONAL INFORMATION

Calories ...... .346 Sugars .... .27g
Protein .... .7g Fat .... .24g
Carbohydrate ...27g Saturates ...... .15g

 40 mins   0 mins

SERVES 4

INGREDIENTS

14 oz/400 g canned mangoes in syrup

2 pieces preserved ginger, chopped

1 cup heavy cream

4 tsp powdered gelatin

2 tbsp hot water

2 egg whites

1½ tbsp light brown sugar

preserved ginger and lime zest,
  to decorate

3  **5**  **6**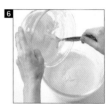

1 Drain the mangoes, reserving the syrup. Blend the mango pieces and ginger in a food processor or blender for 30 seconds, or until smooth.

2 Measure the mango puree and make up to 1¼ cups with the reserved mango syrup.

3 In a separate bowl, whip the cream until it forms soft peaks. Fold the mango mixture into the cream, until well combined.

4 Dissolve the gelatin in the hot water and let cool slightly.

5 Pour the gelatin into the mango mixture in a steady stream, stirring. Cool in the refrigerator for 30 minutes, until almost set.

6 Beat the egg whites in a clean bowl until they form soft peaks, then beat in the sugar. Gently fold the egg whites into the mango mixture with a metal spoon.

7 Spoon the mousse into individual serving dishes, decorate with preserved ginger and lime zest, and serve.

COOK'S TIP

The gelatin must be stirred into the mango mixture in a gentle, steady stream to prevent it from setting in lumps when it comes into contact with the cold mixture.

Exotic Fruit Crêpes

These crêpes are filled with an exotic array of tropical fruits. Decorate lavishly with edible flowers or mint sprigs.

NUTRITIONAL INFORMATION	
Calories 382	Sugars 24g
Protein 7g	Fat 17g
Carbohydrate . . .53g	Saturates 3g

🍐 🍐 🍐

🍮 40 mins   🕐 35 mins

SERVES 4

I N G R E D I E N T S

BATTER

generous 1 cup all-purpose flour

pinch of salt

1 egg

1 egg yolk

1¼ cups coconut milk

4 tsp vegetable oil, plus extra for cooking

FILLING

1 banana

1 papaya

juice of 1 lime

2 passion fruit

1 mango, peeled, pitted, and sliced

4 lychees, pitted and halved

1–2 tbsp honey

edible flowers or sprigs of fresh mint, to decorate

1 Sift the flour and salt into a bowl. Make a well in the center and add the egg, egg yolk, and a little of the coconut milk. Gradually draw the flour into the egg mixture, beating well, and gradually adding the remaining coconut milk to make a smooth batter. Stir in the oil. Cover and chill for 30 minutes.

2 Peel and slice the banana and place in a bowl. Peel and slice the papaya, discarding the seeds. Add to the banana with the lime juice and mix well. Cut the passion fruit in half and scoop out the flesh and seeds into the fruit bowl. Add the mango, lychees, and honey, and stir in.

3 Heat a little oil in a 6-inch/15-cm skillet. Pour in just enough of the crêpe batter to cover the bottom of the pan and tilt so that it spreads thinly and evenly. Cook until the crêpe is just set and the underside is lightly browned, then turn it over and briefly cook the other side. Remove from the skillet and keep warm. Repeat with the remaining batter to make a total of 8 crêpes.

4 To serve, place a little of the prepared fruit filling along the center of each crepe and then roll it into a cone shape. Lay the crêpes, seam side down, on warmed serving plates, decorate with flowers or mint sprigs, and serve.

Coconut Cream Molds

Smooth, creamy, and refreshing—these tempting little custards are made with an unusual combination of coconut milk, cream, and eggs.

NUTRITIONAL INFORMATION

Calories 288	Sugar 24g
Protein 4g	Fat 20g
Carbohydrate ...25g	Saturates 14g

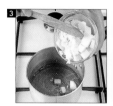

 10 mins   45 mins

SERVES 8

INGREDIENTS

CARAMEL

scant ¾ cup granulated sugar

¾ cup water

CUSTARD

1¼ cups water

3¼ oz/90 g creamed coconut, chopped

2 eggs

2 egg yolks

1½ tbsp superfine sugar

1¼ cups light cream

TO SERVE

sliced banana or slivers of fresh pineapple

1–2 tbsp freshly grated or shredded coconut

1 Have ready 8 small ovenproof dishes of about ⅔-cup capacity. To make the caramel, place the granulated sugar and water in a pan and heat gently to dissolve the sugar, then boil rapidly, without stirring, until the mixture turns a rich golden brown.

2 Immediately remove the pan from the heat and dip the bottom into a bowl of cold water to prevent the caramel from cooking farther. Quickly but carefully divide the caramel among the ovenproof dishes to coat the bottoms.

3 To make the custard, place the water in the same pan as you used for the caramel, add the coconut, and heat, stirring constantly, until the coconut dissolves. Place the eggs, egg yolks, and sugar in a bowl and beat well with a fork. Add the hot coconut milk and stir well to dissolve the sugar. Stir in the cream and strain the mixture into a pitcher.

4 Arrange the dishes in a roasting pan and fill with enough cold water to come halfway up the sides of the dishes. Pour the custard mixture over the caramel

in the dishes, cover with kitchen foil, and cook in a preheated oven, 300°F/150°C, for about 40 minutes, or until set.

5 Remove the dishes, let cool, then chill overnight. To serve, run a knife around the edge of each dish and turn out onto a serving plate.

6 Serve with slices of banana or slivers of fresh pineapple sprinkled with freshly grated or shredded coconut.

Banana & Mango Tart

Bananas and mangoes are a great combination of colors and flavors, especially when topped with toasted coconut chips.

NUTRITIONAL INFORMATION

Calories	235	Sugars	........17g
Protein	.........4g	Fat	..........10g
Carbohydrate	...35g	Saturates	.......5g

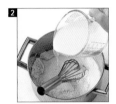

1¼ hrs   5 mins

SERVES 8

INGREDIENTS

8-inch/20-cm ready-made pastry shell

FILLING

2 small ripe bananas

1 mango, sliced

3½ tbsp cornstarch

6 tbsp raw sugar

1¼ cups soy milk

⅔ cup coconut milk

1 tsp vanilla extract

toasted coconut chips, to decorate

1 Slice the bananas and arrange half of them in the pastry shell with half of the mango pieces.

2 Put the cornstarch and sugar in a pan and mix together. Gradually, whisk in the soy milk and coconut milk until combined. Simmer over low heat, whisking constantly, for 2–3 minutes, until the mixture thickens.

3 Stir in the vanilla extract, then spoon the mixture over the fruit.

4 Top with the remaining fruit and toasted coconut chips. Chill in the refrigerator for 1 hour before serving.

COOK'S TIP

Coconut chips are available in some supermarkets and most health food stores. They are worth using because they look more attractive and are not so sweet as dry shredded coconut.

Almond Trifles

Amaretti cookies made with ground almonds have a high fat content. Use cookies made from apricot kernels for a lower fat content.

NUTRITIONAL INFORMATION	
Calories 241	Sugars 23g
Protein 9g	Fat 6g
Carbohydrate . . .35g	Saturates 2g

🧊 1¼ hrs   🕐 0 mins

SERVES 4

INGREDIENTS

8 amaretti cookies

4 tbsp brandy or Amaretto liqueur

1⅓ cups raspberries

1¼ cups lowfat custard

1¼ cups lowfat, plain, thick yogurt

1 tsp almond extract

2 tbsp sliced almonds, toasted

1 tsp unsweetened cocoa

1 Place the cookies in a mixing bowl and, using the end of a rolling pin, carefully crush them into small pieces.

2 Divide the crushed cookies among 4 serving glasses. Sprinkle over the brandy or liqueur and set aside for about 30 minutes to soften.

3 Top with a layer of raspberries, reserving a few for decoration, and spoon over enough custard just to cover.

4 Combine the yogurt with the almond extract and spoon the mixture over the custard, smoothing the surface. Chill in the refrigerator for about 30 minutes.

5 Before serving, sprinkle with the toasted almonds and dust with unsweetened cocoa.

6 Decorate the trifles with the reserved raspberries and serve immediately.

VARIATION

Try this trifle with assorted summer fruits. If they are a frozen mix, use them frozen and let them thaw so that the juices soak into the cookie layer—it will taste delicious.

Mini Florentines

Serve these cookies at the end of a meal with coffee, or arrange in a shallow presentation box for an attractive gift.

NUTRITIONAL INFORMATION	
Calories 75	Sugars 6g
Protein 1g	Fat 5g
Carbohydrate 6g	Saturates 2g

30 mins   10–12 mins

MAKES 40

INGREDIENTS

⅓ cup butter, plus extra for greasing

⅓ cup superfine sugar

2 tbsp golden raisins or raisins

2 tbsp chopped candied cherries

2 tbsp chopped candied ginger

1 oz/25 g sunflower seeds

¾ cup slivered almonds

2 tbsp heavy cream

6 oz/175 g dark or light chocolate

1 Grease and flour 2 cookie sheets or line with baking parchment.

2 Place the remaining butter in a small pan and heat gently until melted. Add the sugar, stir until dissolved, then bring the mixture to a boil. Remove from the heat and stir in the golden raisins, cherries, ginger, sunflower seeds, and almonds. Mix well, then beat in the cream.

3 Place small teaspoons of the fruit and nut mixture onto the prepared cookie sheets, allowing plenty of space for the mixture to spread. Bake in a preheated oven, at 350°F/180°C, for 10–12 minutes, or until light golden in color.

4 Remove from the oven and, whilst still hot, use a circular cookie cutter to pull in the edges to form perfect circles. Let cool and go crisp before removing from the cookie sheet.

5 Break the chocolate into pieces, place in a heatproof bowl over a pan of hot water, and stir until melted. Spread most of the chocolate onto a sheet of baking parchment. When the chocolate is on the point of setting, place the cookies flat-side down on the chocolate and let it harden completely.

6 Cut around the florentines and remove from the baking parchment. Spread a little more chocolate on the coated side of the florentines and use a fork to mark waves in the chocolate. Let set. Arrange the florentines on a plate (or in a presentation box for a gift) with alternate sides facing upward. Keep cool.

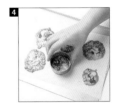

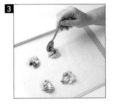

Apple Fritters

These apple fritters are coated in a light, spiced batter and deep-fried until crisp and golden. Serve warm with this unusual almond sauce.

NUTRITIONAL INFORMATION

Calories	438	Sugars	........15g
Protein	.........6g	Fat	..........32g
Carbohydrate	...35g	Saturates	.......4g

🍧 15 mins   🕐 15 mins

SERVES 4

I N G R E D I E N T S

¾ cup all-purpose flour

pinch of salt

½ tsp ground cinnamon

¾ cup warm water

4 tsp vegetable oil

2 egg whites

2 eating apples, peeled

vegetable oil or sunflower oil, for deep-frying

superfine sugar and cinnamon,
   to decorate

A L M O N D   S A U C E

⅔ cup unsweetened yogurt

½ tsp almond extract

2 tsp clear honey

4 Using a sharp knife, cut the apples into chunks and dip the pieces of apple into the batter to coat.

5 Heat the oil for deep-frying to 350°F/180°C, or until a cube of bread browns in 30 seconds. Cook the apple pieces, in batches if necessary, for about 3–4 minutes, until they are light golden-brown and puffy.

6 Remove the apple fritters from the oil with a slotted spoon and drain on absorbent paper towels.

7 Mix together the superfine sugar and the cinnamon and sprinkle over the warm fritters.

8 Mix the sauce ingredients in a serving bowl and serve with the fritters.

1 Sift the flour and salt together into a large mixing bowl.

2 Add the cinnamon and mix well. Stir in the warm water and vegetable oil to make a smooth batter.

3 Whisk the egg whites until stiff peaks form and fold into the batter.

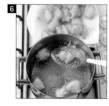